D1661322

VĀKYA-VRITTI

OM

TAT SAT

UNDERSTANDING 'THAT THOU ART'

Shankara Āchārya's

VĀKYA-VRITTI

Translated with a commentary

by

Hari Prasad Shastri

Shanti Sadan
London

First published 2012

29 Chepstow Villas
London W11 3DR

www.shantisadan.org

ISBN 978-0-85424-066-1

Printed and bound in Malta by Gutenberg Press Limited.

INTRODUCTION

The highest ideal of life is the realization of God, the ultimate Reality, in one's soul. Any other thing in the world is secondary and subsidiary. This is the only goal on the attainment of which all doubts cease forever and undisturbable peace within and without is acquired. The inner eyes which see the truth are opened, and man becomes godlike, if not God Himself. Unless this ideal is accepted, a study of Indian philosophy has little meaning. We accept it wholly and entirely: to us it is most reasonable and logical, and it is confirmed by the experience of our holy predecessors such as Shri Dada Bhagavan, Swami Mangalnathji, Swami Rama Tirthaji and others.

Man is not man unless he follows the path of virtue and righteousness called dharma and devotes himself selflessly to the good of others. This fact is confirmed by modern psychology. But dharma is not enough. What is essential is that man's true perceiving faculty, called prajñā, should be awakened, and that he should realize the identity of his local consciousness with the absolute consciousness called truth, awareness and bliss.

How can this be achieved? The heart must be stilled and purified; peace must reign within and without; all narrowness of limitations, egoistic or national, based on a particular creed or religion, must be abandoned in favour of God, the universal spirit, the one and only reality pervading all, animating all and controlling all.

Then follows the process called listening to the truth from a competent and traditional spiritual teacher. This truth must be based on holy Shruti (the revealed scriptures, particularly the Upanishads) and not on the dialectics of Hegel, Kant, Plato or Aristotle.

Finally the man has to cogitate on the spirit of the truth he has listened to. All possible objections are raised and resolved in the light of reason. This is the ultimate stage of the process called living the truth through contemplation under all circumstances. This is nididhyāsana.

The classic which we offer in translation is a series of nididhyāsanas. In a calm and quiet mind rooted in faith in Guru and Govinda (God), the disciple with a strong will to virtue reads these verses one by one and realizes their meaning in his own spirit. He dwells on them single-mindedly and lets their sense permeate the whole of his mental life.

It is not a purely logical treatise. People often ask what to meditate on, what to contemplate. Here is a treatise by the greatest of our Āchāryas, Shri Bhagavatpāda Shankara. It is an invaluable gift of the holy master, and anybody who practises contemplation in the spirit of these verses will have peace within and goodwill towards all living beings, and finally spiritual illumination, which will break the bonds of all limitations.

Hari Prasad Shastri
9th January 1956

Note: Some of the later verses, translated by Dr Shastri but without commentary, have been supplemented by notes based on traditional sources, especially *The Thousand Teachings, Naishkarmya Siddhi* and *Panchadashi*. In these cases the comments are introduced as a 'Note'.

TOPICS

UNDERSTANDING 'THAT THOU ART'
(VĀKYA-VRITTI)
by Shankara Āchārya

Opening Salutations

Verse 1

sarga-sthiti-pralaya-hetum acintya-śaktiṃ
viśveśvaraṃ vidita-viśvam ananta-mūrtim
nirmukta-bandhanam apāra-sukhāmbu-rāśiṃ
śrī vallabhaṃ vimala-bodha-dhanaṃ namāmi

To Him who is the sole cause of the genesis, preservation and withdrawal of the world, who is the only ruler of the universe, who assumes phenomenally the form of the universe of endless multiplicity, who is omniscient, infinite, without any limitation, who is an ocean of limitless bliss, who is the pure realization in its massed form—to that Lord of all prosperity and happiness I offer my salutations.

Contrary to the erroneous interpretation of Deussen and his Indian followers, the Absolute (Brahman) of Vedānta is not 'almost nothingness'; it is positive, negative and yet transcendental. In this verse, which is meant to be a text for serious meditation by students of Vedānta, the holy Āchārya describes some aspects of the Absolute. We must meditate on Brahman as described in this verse, and then, when our reflection is ripe, we will realize the nectar of bliss in this very life.

One of the highest practices for the realization of the ideal of Vedānta is the reflective repetition of 'I am Shiva, the highest good'. It is not something to be grafted on to the immature mind, but it is the realization of the highest good, which is man's Self. This verse contains the meaning of the word 'Shiva'. The aspirant should take into his mind that part of the verse which enumerates the attributes given to the Lord by the human mind and identify his own soul with them. The higher form of adoration is identification with the object of meditation. When the mind becomes one with the object which it reflects upon, it is merged in the object as a wave, rising from the water, ultimately subsides in it.

Mere mechanical repetition of 'I am Shiva' is not very useful; it must be reflective and meditative. To keep the controlled mind on the best and the highest, the yogi meditates on 'I am He, He am I'. This verse gives a method of realization. It is a way to inner peace. It is the best exercise. Brahman is called here 'the Lord of Shrī'. The word 'Shrī' is taken by some commentators to mean Lakshmī, the goddess of prosperity. The meaning is that He is the source and giver of all prosperity—that is, joy, peace, virtue and illumination. This verse can be interpreted both in abstract terms and in terms of the conception of Shrī Vishṇu found in the philosophy of Shrī Rāmānuja Āchārya.

Verse 2

yasya prasādād aham eva viṣnur
mayy eva sarvaṃ parikalpitaṃ ca
itthaṃ vijānāmi sadā ''tma-rūpaṃ
tasyāṅghri-padmaṃ praṇato 'smi nityam

To Him by whose grace I realize that I am Vishṇu (the all-pervading Lord), that the whole universe is imagined in me and that all this is nothing but my own true Self in nature—before His lotus feet I prostrate myself all the time.

One of the cardinal doctrines of the philosophy of Advaita is that the final knot of nescience is cut by the grace of the Lord. Man must do his best by way of discipline, study and the practice of benevolence. When his heart is freed from worldly agitation and from the desires for pleasure and success in the world, the Lord illumines it with the ray of His light and the jīva (individualized soul) acquires realization of Self. Then follows the state of jīvan-mukti (liberation), which the holy Āchārya refers to in this verse. What is the nature of this realization? That this whole universe, internal and external, is imagined in me; that it is in fact nothing but my own nature.

There is a school in Vedānta which believes in the complete efficacy of one's own efforts and places no reliance on the grace of the Lord. This is not the doctrine of the Advaita of Shri Shankara, and such a doctrine can hardly ever give real peace.

It is an element of man's nature to seek the support of somebody or something in his life. In the holy Advaita, the main support of man is the all-pervading reality called Shri Vishṇu. Recognition of this fact is a matter of great consolation. Besides, this is a real way to the reduction and final elimination of the empirical egoity which is the root of all pleasure-seeking and bondage in sansāra (the world). There is no duality involved because in the ultimate stage of meditation the whole universe is revealed as the nature of the Self and nothing else.

The approach to the Teacher

Verse 3

tāpa-trayārka-santaptaḥ kaścid udvigna-mānasaḥ
śam'ādi sādhanair yuktaḥ sad-guruṃ pariprcchati

A certain aspirant who was conscious of the afflictions caused by the extreme heat of the threefold sufferings and was agitated and restless in his mind, acquired the disciplinary qualifications of self-control and so forth, and, approaching his master, asked as follows:

Every man in the realm of relativity called avidyā is subject to the threefold sufferings arising from physical, mental and unknown causes. No one in the world can be free from them. Sometimes there is a slight respite from sufferings and man begins to think that he is happy, but his happiness fades like the dewdrops in the morning sun. Is this suffering essential? Yes. It is an indication of the fact that there is a realm of absolute reality where causation does not function, and that there alone is real rest and peace and bliss.

Is not this life merely a series of sufferings and nothing more? No, because man instinctively thinks to remove his sufferings. He is subconsciously aware of a region where there is peace and bliss, equanimity and joy. Sufferings cause perplexity of the mind. Man sometimes examines the means which lead to the extinction of sufferings, but then the mind produces doubts, bad reasoning and a perpetual hankering after the pleasures of the flesh. He forgets the spiritual yearning and tries to extract the cool water of wisdom from the sands of the life of the senses. Wisdom means disciplining the mind, acquiring inner poise and peace, and having a burning desire to be free from nescience.

The mere wish to be acquainted with the philosophy of Vedānta is not enough. It must be accompanied by the disciplinary qualifications such as self-control, friendliness towards all, pursuit of truth at any cost and higher devotion to God. It is quite useless to study Vedānta merely academically without cultivating these disciplinary qualifications. Unless a man is master of himself, he cannot rise to the higher region of the Absolute. If a bird has stones tied to its feet, it cannot fly in the infinite blue.

Similarly a man steeped in desires for the sense-objects, pursuing the pleasures of power, sex and possession, is doomed to failure.

But there are some rare souls who are blessed with wisdom because of the selfless service they have done to their fellow-men in the past. Such people acquire the qualifications which lead to their candidature for the bliss of the spirit. Once qualified, a man comes to a teacher and asks for his instructions.

Verse 4

anāyāsena yenāsmān mucyeyaṃ bhava-bandhanāt
tan me saṃkṣipya bhagavan kevalaṃ kṛpayā vada

Tell me in brief, O Lord, from thy compassion alone, how I may break from this bondage of being and becoming without undue effort.

People try to get rid of their pain and suffering, but the things of the world go in pairs of opposites. Tears will be followed by smiles, and smiles by tears. Every joy has hidden in it the germ of reaction in the form of grief. No grief is undiluted, as the soul of man loves peace, creative repose and, most of all, inner enlightenment. The natural question is not how to be happy but how to eradicate the causes which lead to the continuation of the process of becoming. As long as becoming continues, man will be a pendulum between a smile and a tear. There is no success in the world in which there is no danger of failure today or tomorrow. Besides, death sits like a sphinx and mocks our efforts, which will surely one day end in nothingness.

What should a man of understanding do? He must remember that there is a way out of this dilemma, that man is not born to be the food of grief and woe. There have been and always are men who have conquered the limitations of birth and death through inner enlightenment and are engaged in liberating others from the darkness of nescience.

Such people are called Gurus. Those who seek, find them. It is not the critic but the man of faith, who has served his fellow-men and has evolved in himself a great urge to be free, who finds them. The word 'Guru' means the one who removes the aspirant from darkness into the region of light. They must be approached with humility and affection, service and adoration.

There is no material fee for the instructions in inner illumination. The only way of return is loving service and a desire to help mankind. The question in this verse is asked of the Guru. Unless a pot is empty it cannot be filled with another precious fluid. The mind must be emptied of earthly ambitions, hate and egoity, and then the teacher can pour into it the rays of the light of truth.

Verse 5

gurur uvāca

> sādhvī te vacana-vyaktiḥ pratibhāti vadāmi te
> idaṃ tad iti vispaṣṭaṃ sāvadhāna-matiḥ śṛṇu

The teacher said:

> Thy speech, as it appears to me, is good and gentle. I will tell thee the secret. I shall clearly explain all that thou needest know. Do thou give attentive hearing to me.

The master approves of the approach of the disciple to him. He is convinced of his sincerity, gentleness and real spirit of enquiry. He promises to impart the full secret to him. He is sure that the speech of the disciple is sincere, and all that he demands now is his undivided attention. Divided attention makes even a worldly end difficult of achievement. Even study of grammar, rhetoric or science needs full attention. Attention is something creative. Any subject which may appear difficult today will reveal its secret to the student when studied with full attention. This advice of the teacher is the key to the understanding of the holy philosophy.

Study of the 'great sentences' (mahā-vākyas) such as 'That thou art' is the sole means to liberation

Verse 6

tat-tvam-asyādi vākyottham̐ yaj jīva-paramātmanoḥ
tādātmya-viṣayaṃ jñānaṃ tad idaṃ mukti-sādhanam

The only means of release from all limitations is the knowledge of the identity of the individual consciousness with Brahman. This knowledge is born of the study of the great sentences such as 'That thou art'.

This is an important verse. It does not prescribe a long and circuitous course of study. It is not like the philosophy of Hegel, little of which can be fully understood even by those who have studied it for twenty years. Bondage, including birth, death, misery and suffering, is dispelled by knowledge. When we use the word 'knowledge' here, we do not mean epistemology, ontology or scientific learning, but the knowledge contained in the short aphorisms such as 'That thou art'.

Over-fondness for speculative knowledge is considered a cause of bondage. If one wants to be an Āchārya or a competent teacher of the spiritual yoga to the intellectual class of people, then a deeper knowledge of philosophy is essential in order to explain to them the meaning of the great sentences. But if one just wants to be freed from the illusion and to help those of normal intellectual ability who are sincere seekers after the spiritual truth, then a knowledge of philosophy, logic and rhetoric is not essential, because the illusion can be removed by the direct flashes of knowledge imparted in the short great sentences (mahā-vākyas) of the Veda. One of these sentences is 'That thou art'.

Verse 7

śiṣya uvāca

ko jīvaḥ kaḥ paraś c'ātmā tādātmyaṃ vā kathaṃ tayoḥ
tat-tvam-asyādi vākyaṃ vā kathaṃ tat pratipādayet

The disciple said:

What is the jīva (the individualized consciousness)? What is the highest Self? How is the identity of the two to be accepted? In what way do the holy texts such as 'That thou art' explain this?

It has been established once for all that the cause of suffering of any kind, whether physical or mental or psychic, is nescience, a want of true understanding of the nature of the Self and of the identity of the microcosmic and macrocosmic aspects of consciousness. This is the cardinal doctrine of Vedānta.

Some will say: 'Is not the performance of good and benevolent deeds enough? Is not the life of prayer, devotion and renunciation sufficient to terminate all man's troubles? Is not the Heaven above this earth, where the faithful go, the only place of eternal rest, peace and happiness?' The reply is: 'No, no!' These states may give a temporary freedom from limitations, but they cannot give absolute freedom. The pleasures and delights of the Paradise of Allah and the Christian Heaven are all limitations: they cannot be eternal because they are subject to achievement. The whole question is, are sufferings real? If they are, then their elimination is impossible, just as the real nature of fire is heat and you cannot have fire without heat. If they are not real, then they must be imaginary and illusory. In this case the only remedy is knowledge of truth.

The Vedāntic position is most logical and is based on experience. The main source of knowledge is the statement in the holy Shruti 'That thou art'. The expression looks unacademic, but its real meaning cannot be understood unless the mind is purged of all earthly desires and uplifted by benevolence, devotion and prayer. These practices are preparatory to the understanding of 'That thou art'.

Verse 8

gurur uvāca

> atra brūmaḥ samādhānaṃ ko 'nyo jīvas tvam eva hi
> yas tvaṃ pṛcchasi māṃ ko 'haṃ brahmaivāsi na saṃśayaḥ

The teacher said:

> Listen, I shall explain this to thee. Thou art jīva. That element in thee which asks: 'What am I?' is undoubtedly Brahman.

There are two phases of consciousness in man. One is

the empirical and the other the transcendental. One is the surface, and the other the rock-bottom truth. When man asks: 'What am I?' he is dimly conscious of his limitations and, although he is the Absolute in reality, is in ignorance of the great truth – this is the superficial view of the reality in man; but the element which asks: 'What am I?' is none other than the Absolute (Brahman), God Himself.

Let it be noted that the statement of the holy Āchārya is in the present tense. The Āchārya says: 'Thou *art* Brahman'. It does not mean that today you are jīva but in the course of time you will become Brahman. It means that without the least doubt, this very moment, the enquiring essence in man is none other than Brahman. This is the grandest truth.

The Sufi conception that man is like a drop in a river seeking union with the sea cannot be interpreted literally. The consciousness in man is, was and ever shall be Brahman, and Brahman only. It is not subject to purification or its opposite. It is neither becoming nor being. Causation has no sway over it. It is made very clear in this text that the individual consciousness in fact is at this very moment Brahman.

The rope is always a rope, though it may appear as a snake owing to an illusion. It never was, is or ever shall be anything other than a rope. It is an error to think: 'Today I am jīva, but when I have obtained samādhi, I will be Brahman.' The best practice for the aspirant is to meditate on 'I am Brahman' not 'I shall be Brahman'.

When philosophy from the time of Plato to Bertrand Russell has been trying to formulate negative and positive aspects of consciousness, the holy Shruti thunders the simple truth in one voice, and it is: 'That thou art'. Science has never been unanimous as to whether reality is matter or spirit. But the spiritual philosophy is different. It says: 'Thou who askest the question "What am I?" art truth, awareness, bliss, and none other.' Immutability is the very nature of consciousness. Let this truth be fully understood by the adherents of the Vedānta. Indeed, who can doubt it in the light of the personal experience of the greatest and holiest of men from Shankara Ācharya to Swami Rama Tirtha?

Verse 9

śiṣya uvāca

> padārtham eva jānāmi nādyāpi bhagavan sphuṭam
> ahaṃ brahmeti vākyārthaṃ pratipadye kathaṃ vada

The disciple said:

> O Lord, I do not yet fully understand the meaning of the words 'I am Brahman'. Will you be gracious enough to enlighten me so that I may grasp the meaning of the whole sentence?

Frankness on the part of the disciple is an essential element of studentship. To give an impression of understanding when the holy truth is inadequately understood is not becoming. There are people who like to say: 'I understand; yes, I know', whereas in fact they have hidden doubts and are unconvinced of the meaning of the great sentences. Such people cannot obtain real benefit from the knowledge imparted by the teacher. The life of a disciple is based on perfect frankness. It is said in a Persian proverb: 'A disciple should be naked, as it were, before the master.'

In this verse the disciple brings out a difficulty and does not hide his ignorance of the real meaning of the truth contained in the great sentence. To say: 'I do not believe it!' is more than stupid; it is dangerous. The man who is so hot-headed and has such erroneous ideas had better withdraw himself from the circle of discipleship. Nobody is eager to convince a sceptic unless he humbly applies for enlightenment. 'Lord, I do not understand it'—this is the right spirit which evokes from the gracious heart of the teacher the real response in the form of light.

First one must grasp the meanings of the words 'That' and 'thou', then of the whole sentence.

Verse 10

gurur uvāca

> satyam āha bhavān atra vigānaṃ naiva vidyate
> hetuḥ padārtha-bodho hi vākyārthāvagater iha

The teacher said:

> Thy words, O honoured one, are true and there is no taint in them. Know that the meaning of the words must

be understood before the meaning of the whole sentence becomes clear.

The holy teacher in reply addresses the disciple as 'Bhavān', which is a Sanskrit word indicative of very high honour. He holds him not only in great affection but also in great esteem. It is true that to have access to the heart of a person who wants to understand the holy truth you have to have affection for him and also reverence. Vulgar people think that affection and respect do not go together, but the tradition of holy Vedānta is to the contrary. Then the teacher pronounces the expression of the disciple to be free from all taint—that is to say, there is no diplomacy about it, no attempt to conceal ignorance, no high-sounding talk and no boasting. The words of the disciple are pure, simple, true and full of reverence. This is to be carefully noted by those who want to conform to the tradition of the holy teachings.

The teacher points out that a sentence, which is a combination of words, can be understood as a whole only when the meanings of the words are made clear. In some cases the meaning of the words is obscure and the sentence is interpreted to suit the policy of the speaker. In the French Revolution the words 'fraternity, equality and liberty' were widely used, but the leaders like Mirabeau, Danton and Robespierre had no intention of upholding these ideals. In our intercourse we must therefore recognize the meaning of the words which are used. This verse is an expression of the Āchārya's deep love of dharma.

Negating the direct meaning of 'thou'

Verse 11

antaḥkaraṇa-tad-vṛtti-sākṣī-caitanya-vigrahaḥ
ānanda-rūpaḥ satyaḥ san kiṃ n'ātmānaṃ prapadyase

Thou art the witness of thy mind (antaḥkaraṇa) and its mutations (vrittis). Thou art of the form of pure consciousness. Being existence and bliss, how art thou not the Self?

The Advaita dictum 'Thou art Brahman' is established by dialectics in this verse. There are two categories in sansāra (the world), the real and the unreal. The unreal is the object, passing and never fixed; whereas the real is the self-luminous, ever-shining light which illumines both the subject and the object, but which in the lower sense may be said to be the subject. In the highest sense we cannot call Brahman a subject.

One cannot deny that there is an individual consciousness. 'I think, I feel, I will, I know', is an undeniable fact. Is the object real? If it is, then the subject, being entirely opposed to it, cannot be real at the same time. If the subject is real, then its qualities such as immutability, blissfulness owing to its being the dearest of all things, and its power of witnessing and revealing all objects cannot be called unreal.

The subject and object are not the same. The individual consciousness which functions as the mental operations is not its own witness. The conclusion is that the Self of man, which shorn of all its mental adjuncts is nothing but pure consciousness, is the same as the consciousness absolute—the cosmic consciousness. If we do not accept this convincing conclusion reached by the dialectics of Shrī Shankara, we will have to relegate the cosmic consciousness to the realm of objectivity and, as such, it will have to be limited, mortal and inert. One does not have to stretch the imagination too far to understand this point of view. Though established by reasoning, the truth is to be known by contemplation and discipline. The supreme test is experience, and the experience of the holy sages and even your own experience establishes the fact: 'That thou art'.

How the supreme spiritual experience of reality arises in the human mind is indicated in the following verse.

Verse 12

satyānanda-svarūpaṃ dhī-sākṣiṇaṃ jñāna-vigraham
cintay'ātmatayā nityaṃ tyaktvā dehādigāṃ dhiyam

Abandoning the mind, which identifies itself with the body and the other adjuncts, meditate steadfastly with faith on the truth that your own Self is the mind's witness, of the form of knowledge, and reality and bliss by nature.

This is the method of meditation by which the Self is realized as reality, bliss and knowledge. It has been remarked that an intellectual conviction of the reality of

Self and its identity with the cosmic Self is not of much value unless realized practically in the mental consciousness. In meditation you do not realize the truth as it is but you negate what it is not, and what remains after the negation of the mind and the body is verily the cosmic consciousness. If the space in the jar is considered in its real form, you will have to negate the roundness which the form of the jar gives to it. What remains when you do this is the cosmic space. The same applies to the Self.

This meditation is not an intellectual process, because in meditation the truth is made real by contemplation: the intellect itself does not operate. After steady contemplation for a long, long time in solitude under the discipline of detachment, devotion and faith, the light of the Self shines through and floods the whole mental consciousness. The world is transformed from a set of limitations into pure consciousness, which is blissful. Without this realization, Vedānta remains merely talk.

Verse 13

rūpādimān yataḥ piṇḍas tato n'ātmā ghaṭādivat
viyad-ādi mahā-bhūta-vikāratvāc ca kumbhavat

The body is not the Self because, like a jar, it has a form and so forth and because, like an earthen pot, it is a modification of the five great elements starting with ether.

It is a grievous mistake to think that the body is the Self.

This error is at the root of countless dangers and endless mischief and harm. The holy Āchārya demolishes this error in a characteristic manner by showing how distinct the body is from the Self.

The Self is formless, is not composed of the physical elements, and does not have the attributes of a physical object. If it were otherwise, you could not attribute immortality or consciousness to it.

Soon after the death of one whom we love, we want to dispose of the body by cremation or otherwise. In order to be immortal, eternal and all bliss, the Self must be distinct from the body which, like a pot, is an object of the senses, is composed of many elements and has qualities of form and so forth. The Self being the subject, nay the witness-self, must be different from the object. If it were an object, then it would be just like an earthen pot and could neither be an object of our utmost endearment nor the receptacle of consciousness.

This line of argument is incontestable. It establishes the immateriality of the spiritual nature of the Self, and should be reflected upon again and again by those who want to know the truth. How mistaken it is to take the body for the Self and to worship it and care only for it! It changes every minute and will one day perish entirely. To consider the body to be the Self will sooner or later cause very great grief.

Verse 14

śiṣya uvāca

> anātmā yadi piṇḍo 'yam ukta-hetu-balān mataḥ
> karāmalakavat sākṣād ātmānaṃ pratipādaya

The disciple said:

> If this body is not the Self, as has been demonstrated by this reasoning, then please be good enough to tell me what the Self is. I want the matter to be as plain as a gooseberry on the palm of the hand.

It has been established by incontestable reasoning that the body is not the Self. The arguments of Chārvāka, who maintained that the body was the Self, are as hollow as the clear sky in autumn. Even a man of little reasoning power can see that the body, which changes every minute and is inert, cannot be the Self, which is sentient, immutable and imperishable. Things which exist and function in the realm of time-space are perishable, and the body is no exception to this rule.

Many of the Tang emperors tried to make their bodies immortal by resorting to the Taoist elixir, but they died all the same. An Indian pundit, who claimed to have discovered the secret of physical immortality, came to China and offered to disclose it to the Tang emperor. The elixir was prepared with great care, but the pundit died the same night its preparation was completed. The chief value of life is that it can be a means to realize the immortality of the spirit consciously; all attempts to immortalize the body will fail miserably.

What is the Self? How are we to know that it is immortal and imperishable? These questions are natural and much of our peace depends on answering them. If there is no immortal element in the human personality, then all attempts to achieve the high ethical ideal and that of mysticism are bound to fail. In the following verse the holy Āchārya reveals the secret of the Self.

Verse 15

gurur uvāca

> ghaṭa-draṣṭā ghāṭād bhinnaḥ sarvathā na ghaṭo yathā
> deha-draṣṭā tathā deho nāham ity avadhāraya

The teacher said:

> The seer of the pot is ever different from the pot, its object, and is never one with the pot. Similarly, the seer of the body is ever different from the body, its object. Therefore the truth is: 'I am not the body'; this you must understand.

Over two thousand years ago the Greek philosopher established that the subject is ever different from the object. This rule has ever since been accepted by all thinking people. It is clear that the tree which I see is not myself; it is an object and I am the subject, each being radically different from the other. If this rule is not accepted, there is no place for logic and reason. The holy Āchārya begins the brilliant introduction to his commentary on the *Brahma Sūtras* with this premise, and every student who bears it in mind will find Shrī Shankara easy to follow.

Verse 16

evam indriya-dṛṅ nāham indriyāṇīti niścinu
mano buddhis tathā prāṇo nāham ity avadhāraya

The same argument shows that I, who am the witness of the senses, am not the senses. Thus I am not the mind, intellect or vital force; this you must understand.

The same argument leads to the conclusion that the Self is different from the senses and the mind. That which says 'my mind, my eyes, my speech', is different from the mind, the eyes and speech. Our whole life and happiness depend on what we think ourselves to be. If the Self is something which is subject to change or momentary sensations, as one school of Buddhists think, then we can never find rest and peace in the world.

Change and action are in the mind and the body. If they were natural to the Self of man, he would have no desire for rest or peace and a holiday. Pundit Baijnath used to say: 'The real rest of the soul is in actionlessness; but action will continue to exist in the mind and the body, and to expect them to be without action is to expect the impossible.' When it is said in the *Bhagavad Gītā*: 'O Arjuna, be established in the Self', the meaning is that the Self should be detached from the mind and the body by study and contemplation, and then the Self can rest in itself. Consciousness is a property neither of the mind nor of the Self. That the Self is the receptacle of consciousness (and not consciousness itself) is the Nyāya and not the Advaita doctrine.

The highest and ideal endeavour of man is to realize the Self as pure consciousness, free from all attributes and action. Such a Mahātma does not live like a stone. He works all the time to set an example of goodness to others, but he knows in his own consciousness that he is actionless and attributeless. The highest meditation and truest affirmation is: 'I am Shiva'.

If man is not the spirit, which is pure consciousness and nothing else, then there can be no such thing as release or even respite from the agonies of the mind and the senses.

Verse 17

saṅghāto 'pi tathā nāham iti dṛśya-vilakṣaṇam
draṣṭāram anumānena nipuṇaṃ sampradhāraya

Neither am I the aggregate of the senses and the mind. Come to a clear conviction through reasoning (anumāna) that the seer is distinct from the seen.

That the Self is a combination of the mind and the senses is a plausible theory, but it is untrue. Some of the old philosophers inclined to this view. Hegel held the spirit to be absolute, but to him the manifestation of the spirit in the form of the world was more important than the spirit itself. Only the Vedānta of Shrī Shankara declares the truth boldly, and it is that the Self is not a combination of the mind and the senses. Reasoning may help this understanding but the real riddle is solved through contemplation and discipline. The grace of God comes to those who work for it and not to those who only reason and reason, like Berkeley or John Stuart Mill.

Affirming the indirect meaning of 'thou'

Verse 18

dehendriyādayo bhāvā hānādi vyāpṛti-kṣamāḥ
yasya sannidhi-mātreṇa so 'ham ity avadhāraya

That by whose proximity the body, the senses and other such objects acquire the power to act, to select and to differentiate—that am I. This you must understand.

Having established by reasoning that the Self is neither the mind nor the senses, nor a combination of the two, the holy Āchārya now says something positive about the Self. The Self does not and cannot allow of a direct description, because such descriptions are in the realm of relativity and, as such, would condition that which they describe; nevertheless, in this verse, the Āchārya throws out a hint as to the real nature of the Self.

Just as by the proximity of a magnet, iron filings acquire activity, and by the proximity of the sun's rays, the earth becomes fertile, so by the mere proximity of Purusha (the spirit or real Self) prakriti (matter or nature) changes and goes into modifications. This is the Sāṅkhya view, but the Advaita view is slightly different. It is not due to the mere proximity of the Self, although in a sense this is so, but rather due to the omnipotent will of the Lord, expressed macrocosmically as the world and microcosmically as the individual self or jīva, that the mind acquires the power to feel, to imagine, to reason, to will and so forth.

It may be said: 'If the Lord is the real doer, why blame the jīva for any of his acts which may be contrary to dharma?' The explanation is that the individualized consciousness (jīva) suffers from a deluded feeling of identity with the prakriti or māyā, which is the cause of suffering and limitations. The jīva has to be awakened to the spiritual wisdom, and then the actions of the mind and the senses will accord with the universal scheme for the evolution of prakriti and the release of all jīvas from the delusion of duality. There is no fatalism in the holy philosophy.

Verse 19

anāpanna-vikāraḥ sann ayaskāntavad eva yaḥ
buddhy-ādīṃś cālayet pratyak so 'ham ity avadhāraya

That innermost Self which, changeless by nature, puts in motion the intellect and so forth, as the lodestone the iron—that am I. This you must understand.

Here is the cardinal truth of the Advaita philosophy. The Self, which is one, universal and all-pervasive, is the ultimate reality. It is not inert or remote, like the Absolute of Hegel. It contains within it all potentialities, and imparts activity to the mind, intellect, will and emotions. Neither mind nor will is an independent entity; both are dependent upon the Self.

Imagine that the sun is a conscious entity and that it creates the forms and colours in the clouds by its own will; there you have a picture of how the Self, the ultimate reality, which in its lower aspect is associated with the phenomena characterizing nescience (ajñāna), presides over the mind and the intellect. It is called jīva (the individualized consciousness) and is not subordinate to any force. It is an aspect of the Lord omniscient and omnipresent Himself, but as it is self-conditioned, it falls into the error of false identification.

When the stilled mind, devoted to general benevolence and adoration of the Lord, turns its activities on itself by contemplation and meditation, then it realizes its eternal, universal and all-blissful nature. This verse is to be meditated upon. It is self-education of the highest type.

Verse 20

ajaḍātmavad ābhānti yat sānnidhyāj jaḍā api
dehendriya-manaḥ prāṇāḥ so 'ham ity avadhāraya

The Self, the ultimate reality, in whose proximity the body, senses, mind and vital force, though by nature inert, appear to be conscious like the Self—that am I, This you must understand.

According to the Sāṅkhya view, which is recognized in Vedānta, no motion or action can be attributed to the real Self, but prakriti (the primordial substance), by the mere proximity of the Self, assumes motion. This motion is not imparted by an impersonal Self but by that aspect of the Absolute which is omnipotent and omnipresent. It seems puzzling that the Self, which is actionless, should cause motion in prakriti, but the fact is that both prakriti and its motions are phenomenal. If the Self and prakriti were both real, they could not be interdependent or co-existent, for one would be just the same as the other. It is therefore clear that the motions of the mind and the senses are caused by the inner Self, which is nevertheless non-acting.

In the state of deep sleep the mind is actionless, and yet there comes forth from it the dreaming state, in which there is action of many kinds. The dream action is caused by the inner Self which is actionless, but in the ultimate analysis the dream also is unreal and no action has really taken place. The same applies to man's daily action in waking life.

Verse 21

agaman me mano 'nyatra sāmpratam ca sthirī-kṛtam
evaṃ yo vetti dhī-vṛttiṃ so 'ham ity avadhāraya

'My mind had moved elsewhere but now is still.' He who thus knows the vritti of the mind—that am I. This you must understand.

Sometimes the mind is active, sometimes it is at peace; sometimes it is subject to excitement, anger, love or hate, and at other times it is peaceful like the blue sky, in the contemplation of the One-without-a-second. Who is it that cognizes both states of the mind? Who is it that knows that the mind some time ago was active but now is peaceful? Do we not very often say after a meeting in Shanti Sadan: 'Oh, there was real peace in the meeting; I was so happy'? What is that entity which cognizes both the active and the passive state of the mind? It is called Self (Ātman).

Verse 22

svapna-jāgarite suptiṃ bhāvābhāvau dhiyām tathā
yo vetty avikriyaḥ sākṣāt so 'ham ity avadhāraya

He who cognizes the waking, dreaming and sleeping states of consciousness, who is immutable, who witnesses the presence and absence of objects—that am I. This you must understand.

People ask: 'What is Self? What am I?' They often confound Self with mind and attribute the changes of the mind to the Self. Here is a direct explanation of the nature of the Self in so far as it concerns our daily life. The Self is that element in man which knows the presence of objects and also their absence. Objects exist in time and space and are subject to change. No change is possible in the Self, which is the subject of all changes taking place in time and space. Man is either in the waking, dreaming or dreamless sleep state. The waking condition is absent in dream, the dream is absent in dreamless sleep. None of the three states can be the subject of any of the others. Thus it is the Self, called Turīya or the Fourth, which witnesses the three changing conditions of consciousness.

This verse advances a strong reason for establishing the existence of the Self as the witness, which is beyond any change and immortal.

Verse 23

ghaṭāvabhāsako dīpo ghaṭād anyo yatheṣyate
dehāvabhāsako dehī tathā 'haṃ bodha-vigrahaḥ

Just as the light of a lamp which reveals a pot is different from the pot, so I, the embodied Self which reveals the body, being of the form of consciousness, am different from the body.

This is another convincing argument. Let Hume and Locke reason as they like, it is none the less clear that the element in human personality which reveals the body and the mind is neither of them; the revealer is not the revealed. Similarly the Self, which reveals the mind and the body, is not the mind and the body but is different from them. Its nature, too, being imperishable, infinite and immutable, is different from the nature of the body and the mind, which change at every moment. The Buddhist theory that consciousness is a series of moments of change is contradicted in this verse.

These verses are to be meditated upon in perfect silence, physical and mental, and then they will give rise to true Self-consciousness. Intellectual conviction gives no more than a clue to this state.

Verse 24

putra-vittādayo bhāvā yasya śeṣatayā priyāḥ
draṣṭā sarva-priyatamaḥ so 'ham ity avadhāraya

He for whose sake alone son and wealth are loved, the witness, the object of utmost endearment—that am I. This you must understand.

Why do we love the objects of the world? Because they add to the delight of ourselves. It is for the sake of the Self that we love nature, art, friends, study and so forth. Nobody says: 'I love you for the sake of my death.' When we confer affection on any object, we do so, as John Stuart Mill has said, to relieve ourselves of a feeling of want which we would otherwise feel.

Avarice is a great vice, but its origin is misunderstood love of Self; so is love of a dear friend or relative. How often him whom we love today we wish to forsake tomorrow when he no longer promotes our delight! The love of Shri Rāmachandra for truth was an example of self-purification. If the Self can be exalted without the aid of a material object, we grow indifferent to matter, like Newton and other great thinkers. When asked why he sacrificed the privilege of being a high-class and aristocratic Brahmin by loving the untouchables and associating with them, my Guru Shri Dada replied: 'They are my own Self. I cannot feel free or happy unless they are free and happy.'

One of the great conclusions that can be drawn from this verse is that self-exaltation through abstract concentration on virtue and truth gives far greater happiness than love of the concrete, unless it is to serve others. Unless love evokes service, it is a burdensome passion, and it is the service of Self which really matters. Love of letters and philosophy refines the self and makes it lighter: we do not love them for their own sake.

Verse 25

para-premāspadatayā mā na bhūvam ahaṃ sadā
bhūyāsam iti yo draṣṭā so 'ham ity avadhāraya

He who is the seer, who being the object of highest love says: 'May I never suffer extinction, may I always exist' – that am I. This you must understand.

This verse is an explanation of the preceding verse. The first thing that a man has to realize is that he is not the mind; he is just the witness, fundamentally disinterested and detached, and it is in order to promote the happiness and peace of the Self that he loves others. Nobody cares to walk in a thorny wood with bare feet, but we like to see the roses, daffodils and gladioli in the morning as well as in the moonlight because they make us introvertive and unite our mind with the Self within.

One of the arguments in favour of the immortality of the Self is the feeling of the continuity of existence in experience. Those who commit suicide do so because they are tired of the body and circumstances, but not because they are tired of the Self. It is to save the Self from affliction and worries that people resort to suicide, but it is a mistaken idea.

Verse 26

yaḥ sākṣi-lakṣaṇo bodhas tvaṃ-padārthaḥ sa ucyate
sākṣitvam api boddhṛtvam avikāritayā ''tmanaḥ

The meaning of the word 'thou' in the great sentence 'That thou art' is 'the pure knowledge which is the witness'. The Self is the witness as well as the knower, because it undergoes no modifications.

This verse is a commentary on the famous dictum 'That thou art', which is the foundation of Vedānta. The word 'thou' does not here mean the mind, but the immutable consciousness which is beyond change. That which changes is perishable because it exists and functions in time and space. The changeless entity is the infinite, imperishable Self, which is the witness of all the changes of the mind and the body, and the word 'thou' in the great sentence (mahā-vākya) under consideration refers to that consciousness.

Verse 27

dehendriya-manaḥ-prāṇāhaṃkṛtibhyo vilakṣaṇaḥ
projjhitāśeṣa ṣaḍ-bhāva-vikāras tvaṃ padābhidhaḥ

'Thou' means that entity which is completely free from the changes caused by the six attributes and which is neither the body, nor the senses, nor the mind, nor the vital force, nor the ego.

The six changes referred to in the above statement are birth, separative existence, growth, maturity, decay and death. The Self, being an entity beyond time and space, cannot be the body, senses, mind or ego. The word 'ego' can be rather confusing. It stands for the empirical ego and also for the real ego which imparts ego-hood to the basic part of the mind. The empirical ego, which is referred to in everyday expressions such as 'I go, I come', is not the real ego. The empirical ego is associated with action. The real ego is devoid of all action and attributes.

The word 'thou' in the famous dictum refers to pure consciousness. This verse will be understood more by meditation, called nididhyāsana (spiritual contemplation) in Vedānta, than by logical reasoning. There is no higher practice for the realization of the nature of the Self than meditation on these verses of the holy Āchārya.

Negating the direct meaning of 'That'

Verse 28

tvam-artham evaṃ niścitya tad-arthaṃ cintayet punaḥ
atad-vyāvṛtti-rūpeṇa sākṣād vidhi-mukhena ca

Having understood what is implied by the word 'thou', meditate next on the meaning of the word 'That', using the negative method of eliminating what is not 'That' and the positive method based on the direct definition of 'That'.

Two processes of meditation directed to achieving a right understanding of the great dictum 'That thou art' are mentioned in this verse. It is taken for granted that the meaning of the word 'thou', explained in previous verses, has been grasped to some extent. The yogi should then meditate single-mindedly with full concentration on the meaning of the word 'That', with which 'thou' is to be identified. A realization of the identity of the meaning of 'thou' and 'That' leads to the direct cognition of the splendour of the Self, or God, within.

Whilst meditating on 'That', the yogi is asked to consider and reject all that is not directly implied by it, and then to reflect on its real spiritual meaning as given by the holy Āchārya. This is a very useful method of contemplation, which requires the application of intelligence and of the more refined aspect of the mind. It is a method which has something in common with inspiration.

Now the meaning of 'That' is elaborated.

Verse 29

nirastāśeṣa-saṃsāra-doṣo 'sthūlādi lakṣaṇaḥ
adṛśyatvādi guṇakaḥ parākṛta-tamo malaḥ

That which is completely free from the limitations of the phenomenal world and is known by such descriptions as 'neither dense nor subtle', which never has the characteristics of an object and is untouched by the taint of nescience or limitations in any form—that is the supreme Self.

In this verse the holy Āchārya compassionately explains the meaning of the word 'That', which is to be meditated upon. In the Upanishad it is said: 'Not this, not this'. In a higher sense whatever positive statement you make about the Self is in the sphere of the phenomenal world and does not apply to the absolute Self. Our words are meant to express worldly existence and not the spiritual reality.

Sometimes the holy Shruti describes the Self negatively, but very often it is merely hinted at. It is the Guru, established in the divine consciousness, who transmits through his loving compassion what words cannot convey. In the course of meditation let the yogi eliminate all that applies to worldly objects in any form and any sense. Let it be remembered that the Self is not an object. How can the subject be described? When pressed for a definition of Brahman by his beloved wife, the holy sage Yājñavalkya said: 'O dear one, how can the knower be known?' Let the yogi in meditation divest the Self of any limitation and meditate on it as 'I, I, I'. Then he will have the relish of peace and pass into the mental state of tranquillity in which glimpses of Ātman are revealed by the grace of the Guru.

Verse 30

nirastātiśayānandaḥ satya-prajñāna-vigrahaḥ
sattā-sva-lakṣaṇaḥ pūrṇaḥ paramātmeti gīyate

That beyond which there is no higher bliss, which is of the nature of existence-knowledge, which is defined as truth and is perfect—that is the supreme Self.

Here is not a definition but a partial description of the supreme Self, Paramātman (God). In what terms shall we think of Him or It? It is a lower conception to regard Him as the Creator of the universe and Father of all. The metaphysical conception of truth is personal and yet transcendental. The first thing to be noticed is that the highest bliss, which man prizes more than any object in the world and which is the goal of his struggles in the realm of virtue and truth, as in the physical world, is by nature the supreme Self. There are stages in pleasure, some being lower and some higher. The refined man seeks pleasure in art, science and the practice of virtue, but the source of all bliss is the supreme Self which abides in man.

Man does not run after what he knows to be an illusion. He soon forgets a magic show which he has seen. Who tries to catch the end of a rainbow? Who wants to re-experience a pleasant dream? Man loves reality, and that reality is the supreme Self.

Knowledge is the essence of life. It is not the knowledge of an object or concept, but it is that element in man which makes knowledge possible. 'Brahman is that which produces knowledge' is a dictum of the holy metaphysics.

Paramātman is not only bliss and an instrument of knowledge, but also truth. These are not borrowed qualities but are the very nature of the supreme Self. What heat is to fire, bliss, reality and knowledge are to the supreme Self. The lesson of the holy philosophy is that these three, which man loves more than anything else, are the nature of his own Self and are not to be found externally. Let him look for great bliss, reality, knowledge and truth, through the telescope of his purified and restful mind, in his own Self. The highest meditation is: 'I am Shiva', which contains within it the whole meaning of this verse.

Affirming the indirect meaning of 'That'

Verse 31

sarva-jñatvaṃ pareśatvaṃ tathā sampūrṇa-śaktitā
vedaiḥ samarthyate yasya tad brahmety avadhāraya

He whose omniscience, overlordship and omnipotence are spoken of by the Veda is Brahman. This you must understand.

Deussen and other Western interpreters of Vedānta have failed to understand the real nature of the Absolute. We cannot know the nature of the Absolute by the intellect because the intellect functions in the realm of duality and Brahman is non-dual. The intellect analyses, compares and infers, but Brahman cannot be subjected to any of these methods. It is for this reason that the supreme authority on Brahman is scriptural revelation, which is itself subject to verification in personal experience. Logical demonstration is far inferior to experience.

Brahman is omniscience, omnipotence and the supreme Lord of the universe, both macrocosm and microcosm. This is the real nature of the Absolute of Vedānta. In one respect Brahman is beyond mind and speech, but when we consider Him in relation to the world and our daily experience, we ascribe to Him the above-mentioned attributes.

Vedānta is not Buddhistic nihilism. Many pseudo-Vedāntins have failed to understand that Brahman is both omnipotence and omniscience, but this is the bedrock of the Vedāntic ontology. Let us meditate on Him as He is described in this verse and we shall be filled with peace.

Verse 32

yaj jñānāt sarva-vijñānaṃ śrutiṣu pratipāditam
mṛdādy aneka-dṛṣṭāntais tad-brahmety avadhāraya

That by whose knowledge all that is knowable is known, as the Shruti proves by the illustrations of the clay and the pot, is Brahman. This you must understand.

In this verse there are two statements. One is that Shruti is the source of knowledge about Brahman. It not only describes Brahman but also gives many illustrations to explain its nature. The relationship which exists between the clay and the pot made of clay illustrates the nature of Brahman and the universe. When Brahman is known, nothing knowable remains unknown. Just as when you know a lump of gold, you know all the ornaments made of gold, so when you know the cause of the world, Brahman, you have a knowledge of everything in the world. It does not mean that you become clairvoyant or, in the sense of modern theosophists, know what is taking place in the stars or in the imaginary astral world. The meaning is simply this—that since Brahman is the substratum, the main cause of the universe, when you know Him your sense of cognition is satisfied for ever and you do not hanker after any other knowledge.

Many people who have dabbled in Yoga try to know of the mysteries of Orpheus or study the *Tibetan Book of the Dead,* but such knowledge is neither useful nor elevating. It is enough for the wise to know: 'All this is my Self'.

Many parts of his kingdom may be unknown to a king in his conscious self; yet he feels that they belong to him and he knows them. So a knower of Brahman knows all that is knowable as the effect of the ultimate reality. Does not the knowledge of water give a knowledge of all the waves, bubbles and breakers?

Verse 33

yad-ānantyaṃ pratijñāya śrutis tat-siddhaye jagau
tat-kāryatvaṃ prapañcasya tad-brahmety avadhāraya

That to which the Vedas attribute infinity and of which they declare the universe to be the effect in order to bring an understanding of it to the people—that is Brahman. This you must understand.

Here the same fact is emphasized as in the previous verse. The yogi must meditate on Brahman as the infinite. That which goes beyond the limits of time and space and is beyond human understanding is called infinite. This can apply only to Brahman and to nothing else.

Verse 34

vijijñāsyatayā yac ca vedānteṣu mumukṣubhiḥ
samarthyate 'tiyatnena tad-brahmety avadhāraya

That which has been very carefully established in the Vedānta as the only goal for the seekers of final release—that is Brahman. This you must understand.

Here is a further explanation of Brahman to be meditated upon. Although the authority of holy Shruti is unchallenged, reasoning plays a very important part in Vedānta and is applied to silence opposition and to put on a firm logical basis the conception of Brahman, the non-dual reality. True reasoning is not mere logic-chopping but very practical metaphysics.

Over and above all man seeks liberation from limitations. His soul aspires to that unbroken and unsurpassed peace which is called moksha (release). There is no other way to experience that supreme spiritual state than to realize Brahman as the abiding entity in the intellect and the soul of man. Though the grace of God is essential, it is not the direct cause of liberation. His grace enables man to surpass all limitations and to realize the Highest.

Verse 35

jīvātmanā praveśaś ca niyantṛtvaṃ ca tān prati
śrūyate yasya vedeṣu tad-brahmety avadhāraya

That which the Vedas declare to have entered all beings as their individual soul (Jīvātman) and to be their controller—that is Brahman. This you must understand.

This is also a verse for meditation. Brahman is not some powerful dweller in the skies or a transcendent principle as conceived by Immanuel Kant. It is not the God in the Seventh Heaven, but it is the principle of truth and consciousness immanent in each and every being. It is the cause of the individualized soul (jīva). Another thing to be remembered is that it is not a principle which works unconsciously like gravitation. Brahman controls the soul and there is nothing arbitrary in its functions, though it cannot be said to be purely rational. It is a mystery which is understood only when the soul has merged all its limitations in devotion-contemplation and has realized its identity with Brahman.

This verse establishes a great spiritual truth. It demolishes the conceptions of the Buddhists and the followers of Sānkhya. Brahman controls māyā. It is Brahman who dispenses the rewards of actions. Verily there is no other controller than Brahman.

Verse 36

karmaṇāṃ phala-dātṛtvaṃ yasyaiva śrūyate śrutau
jīvānāṃ hetu-kartṛtvaṃ tad-brahmety avadhāraya

That which the holy Shruti declares to be the giver of the fruits of human actions and the cause of man's individual existence—that is Brahman. This you must understand.

Two further reasons are adduced to mature the conviction of the truth about Brahman and the Self. Man acts, and his actions are judged good or otherwise. That power which rewards him for his good actions is Brahman. It cannot be the little self of man. No prisoner would himself go to prison, and no good deed could be rewarded on mere merit without agency. Therefore Brahman is to be understood as that which rewards man for his good deeds. Often good actions seem to lead to distress and trouble, but the reward is ultimate and assured. Life has to be studied on a very long-term view. Besides, who has made the infinite look finite and the cosmic existence assume phenomenal individual existence? By meditating on these facts we come to the conclusion that Brahman exists. Mere logical proofs are not enough. It is by contemplation of this fact in deep silence that we reap the real benefit of shānti (spiritual peace).

Grasping the meaning of the whole sentence

Verse 37

tat-tvam-padārthau nirṇītau vākyārthaś cintyate 'dhunā
tādātmyam atra vākyārthas tayor eva padārthayoḥ

So far the meanings of the words 'That' and 'thou' have been explained. Now we proceed to deal with the meaning of the whole sentence, which consists in the absolute identity of the words 'That' and 'thou'.

The final enlightenment of the individual spirit in its infinite, cosmic and divine aspect takes place when the Guru instructs the disciple, who, by faith, devotion, discipline and service, is fully qualified for instruction in the meaning of the great Vedic dictum 'That thou art'. In previous verses the holy Āchārya has thrown a flood of light on the meanings of the terms 'That' and 'thou' in the holy dictum. Now he attempts to convey the meaning of the whole sentence 'That thou art'.

Man has first to understand what is his own real Self (Ātman). The word 'Ātman' means the inmost reality in man, deeper than which nothing exists in the human personality. It is the real spirit of man. It is the 'thou' by which the Guru conveys the means of enlightenment.

Verse 38

samsargo vā viśiṣṭo vā vākyārtho nātra sammataḥ
akhaṇḍaika-rasatvena vākyārtho viduṣāṃ mataḥ

This great sentence does not imply the co-existence of the individual and the cosmic Self, nor does it mean that a particular aspect of Brahman is the Self. According to the wise, it affirms the basic identity of 'That' and 'thou' without any reservation or condition.

The dualist philosophers are responsible for many distortions of the holy dictum. Some have assumed wrongly, through misinterpretation, that both the Self of man and the divine Self exist together, just as the light of a candle burning by day co-exists with the sunlight. Others hold that the sentence expresses a particular characteristic of the individual Self but not its identity with Brahman. They say for instance, that the Self of man is divine but not the same as God. Rāmānuja, Madhva and Nimbarka have offered their own interpretations of the great sentence on these and similar lines, but wise students do not accept them. In fact the meaning is the whole and absolute identity of 'That' and 'thou' (Brahman and jīva).

When the yogi meditates on the identity of his Self with the divine Self as the one and only reality which is non-dual in character, the truth is revealed to him if he has been a true disciple to his Guru.

Verse 39

pratyag-bodho ya ābhāti so 'dvayānanda-lakṣaṇaḥ
advayānanda-rūpaś ca pratyag-bodhaika-lakṣaṇaḥ

The innermost consciousness of man is the infinite bliss without a second; and the infinite bliss without a second is none other than the innermost consciousness of man.

It may be asked what is the nature of the Self of man, which is pure consciousness and entirely distinct from the body and the mind. The nature of consciousness is infinity and bliss. These two words are synonymous: in infinity there is no discord and no disharmony, and the absence of discord and disharmony means bliss. Being consciousness, the Self is like the endless blue sky or the space in which the universes roll like waves in water. It is nothing but blissfulness. There are no impediments, no obstacles, nothing to achieve, nothing to lose. Ever free from want, the Self of man is pure blissfulness. It cannot be conceived to be otherwise. It is distinction and difference which causes grief and weariness. The bliss of consciousness is not comparable to any other bliss, as it alone exists with nothing else beside it. Such is Ātman or the innermost consciousness of man. This is a rational concept which has to be realized in meditation and in surrender of the individuality and egoity to Guru and Govinda. What greater achievement can man have than realization of his Self?

Verse 40

ittham anyonya-tādātmya-pratipattir yadā bhavet
abrahmatvaṃ tvam-arthasya vyāvarteta tadaiva hi

When the identity of jīva and Brahman is firmly grasped by the intellect, then the erroneous conception that 'thou' means anything other than Brahman will go for ever.

For a long time the candidate to liberation will continue to think that theoretically he may be Brahman but practically he is subject to suffering, loss and so forth. It is therefore necessary that the inner meaning of 'thou' and 'That' should be firmly established. Intellectual understanding is necessary, and for this an intellect set on sattva (purity and light) is essential. It is not like geometry, which even a murderer can understand. Empedocles was a greater philosopher than the Ionians because he postulated the necessity of a pure intellect devoted to divine contemplation for an understanding of the nature of the Self. Charity, tolerance, cheerfulness, endurance and non-egoity must be practised along with attempts to understand the nature of the Self intellectually.

Verse 41

tad-arthasya ca pārokṣyaṃ yadyevaṃ kiṃ tataḥ śṛṇu
pūrṇānandaika-rūpeṇa pratyag-bodho 'vatiṣṭhate

The indirect knowledge of 'That' will also come to an

end. How can you explain this? The answer is that the innermost consciousness in man is by nature the infinite bliss.

In some Shrutis, Brahman is pronounced to be unknowable directly by the mind. Be it so, yet its knowability is evident by reason of the fact that it is infinite bliss in its own nature. In the state of sleep, when the mind and all power of conception and perception is absent, the Self rests in its own bliss, and no want or suffering is experienced at all. From this fact and the experience of samādhi, we infer that, although Ātman cannot be known by the intellect, its nature is bliss and self-evident.

Verse 42

tat-tvam-asyādi vākyaṃ ca tādātmya-pratipādane
lakṣyau tat-tvaṃ-padārthau dvāv upādāya pravartate

Sentences such as 'That thou art' teach the identity of jīva and Brahman by the use of the indirect meanings of 'That' and 'thou'.

Note: The individual self ('thou') and the cosmic Self, Brahman ('That'), appear possessed of contradictory attributes, which preclude their identity. Therefore man has to discard their direct meanings, and seek a deeper meaning that is common to both. Hidden behind the apparent qualities of 'thou' and 'That', is being-consciousness, of the nature of infinite bliss and non-dual.

Verse 43

hitvā dvau śabalau vācyau vākyaṃ vākyārtha-bodhane
yathā pravartate 'smābhis tathā vyākhyātam ādarāt

Thus by rejecting the two direct meanings we carefully show how the sentence reveals its meaning.

Note: Though the spiritual truth transcends reason, in this verse the holy Āchārya shows how reason can prepare the way for the higher intuition. The realization of the supreme wisdom, which is affirmed in such classics as the *Ashtavakra Gita* and the *Avadhut Gita,* is aided by the deep, single-minded enquiry (vichāra) of the one who follows the spiritual discipline. The great sentence 'That thou art' is not a matter to be held on grounds of faith alone, nor is it a magical formula that defies logical scrutiny. The intellect will avoid misconceptions if it approaches the holy dictum on the lines suggested in these verses.

Verse 44

ālambanatayā bhāti yo 'smat pratyaya-śabdayoḥ
antaḥkaraṇa-saṃbhinna-bodhaḥ sa tvaṃ-padābhidhaḥ

That consciousness, conditioned by the mind (antaḥ-karaṇa), which is the foundation of the word and idea 'I', is the direct meaning of the word 'thou'.

Note: What is it in us that says 'I'? Why is it that man feels himself to be the centre of the universe? Here, the pure consciousness in man, which alone confers life and awareness on the body and mind, and is essentially unconditioned, is identified as the basis of the individualized 'I', and forms the direct meaning of 'thou'.

Verse 45

māyopādhir jagad-yoniḥ sarva-jñatvādi-lakṣaṇaḥ
parokṣya-śabalaḥ satyādy ātmakas tat-padābhidhaḥ

The consciousness which, conditioned by māyā, is the womb of the universe, which is characterized by omniscience and so forth, which can be known indirectly, and whose nature is existence, consciousness and bliss, is the direct meaning of the word 'That'.

The word 'That' in 'That thou art' means pure consciousness and also the consciousness self-conditioned by māyā, which is its medium of expression. Māyā has not reduced the real nature of consciousness. Though conditioned, the consciousness yet is omniscience and reality.

There are many scholars who believe that the jīva is an expression of Īshvara (the Lord) who is limited by māyā (his self-conditioning power of illusion, which is ultimately unreal). But let us remember that both jīva and Īshvara indicate pure consciousness, Brahman, and nothing more. We cannot apply to the same thing the state of being cognized and also at the same time of being non-cognized.

Verse 46

pratyak-parokṣataikasya sa-dvitīyatva-pūrṇatā
virudhyate yatas tasmāl lakṣaṇā sampravartate

As the qualities of being directly known and being indirectly known, of being absolute and having a second beside itself, exclude one another in one and the same substance, therefore the indirect meanings have to be taken.

Note: 'That' or Brahman is said to be indirectly known (paroksha), whereas man has direct acquaintance with his self, 'thou', though his knowledge of its true nature is obstructed by his sense of identification with the finite personality. The jīva or individual feels separate and one among many; hence his nature, thus understood, contradicts that of the Absolute, which is 'one-without-a-second'.

Verse 47

mānāntara-virodhe tu mukhyārthasya parigrahe
mukhyārthenāvinābhūte pratītir lakṣaṇocyate

When taking the direct meaning of a word would lead to inconsistency with other data, then a meaning which is evident but not excluded by the direct meaning is called the indirect meaning.

Note: God, or Brahman, is consciousness absolute, and the consciousness in man, partially revealed in his mind, is not separate, in essence, from the supreme consciousness. It is not possible to imagine a plurality of consciousnesses. Multiplicity exists on the mental and physical planes, but not in consciousness itself. The indirect meaning of 'That thou art' relates to the consciousness common to both and which transcends duality.

Verse 48

tat-tvam-asy-ādi vākyeṣu lakṣaṇā bhāga-lakṣaṇā
so 'yam ityādi vākyastha-padayor iva nāparā

The only possible interpretation of sentences such as 'That thou art' is an interpretation based on the omission of inconsistent qualities, just as with the words that compose the sentence 'He is this'.

Note: The sentence 'He is this' is an example of an identity that prevails despite its association with different and contradictory attributes. He, the person seen yesterday in another place and dressed differently, is this, the person seen here now. In establishing the identity of 'He' and 'this', the attributes of time and place have to be excluded.

Practice of mind control, shravana and manana must be continued.

Verse 49

aham brahmeti vākyārtha-bodho yāvad dṛḍhī-bhavet
śam'ādi-sahitas tāvad abhyasec chravaṇādikam

One should practise mental control to the utmost and continue hearing and cogitating, until the deep sense of the sentence 'I am Brahman' is clearly and firmly understood.

Discipline and meditation, as well as devotion to the Lord, are essential until the Self is fully realized. Many people relax their discipline when they begin to study Vedānta and are misled by such ideas as 'Even discipline and devotion are unreal'. They overlook the fact that the unreal is cancelled by unreality and forget the importance of discipline and devotion. It is further to be noted that even after the attainment of jīvan-mukti (liberation in life) one has to continue with discipline and devotion. The freedom of the Jīvan-mukta does not lead him to the realm of nescience. Sattva becomes his very nature and he does not deviate from truth, compassion, devotion and further and further study of the holy truth. In order to set an example to others, Shri Dada used to do his worship and meditation every day for several hours. If there is any joy in the world of limitations, it is in the practice of discipline, dharma and devotion, though this joy, too, is from the Self and not from nescience.

The Jīvan-mukta is liberated from nescience and sansāra.

Verse 50

śruty-ācārya-prasādena dṛḍho bodho yadā bhavet
nirastāśeṣa-saṃsāra-nidānaḥ puruṣas tadā

When the conviction of the truth of the holy dictum is attained by the grace of the teacher and the holy Shruti, then the aspirant is wholly freed from the limitations of sansāra and its cause, nescience.

The greatest prominence is given in the spiritual teachings to the grace of the teacher of Shruti. A teacher of secular knowledge or theosophical mysteries or Hatha Yoga practices is not considered a Guru. A real Guru must be a teacher of the holy Shruti, and the essence of the Shruti is contained in the four great dicta, 'I am Brahman' and so forth. The grace of God flows from the teacher himself. Just as a room in winter is heated by a radiator which has first been heated itself, so the grace of God shines forth through the Self-realized Mahātma who teaches the meaning of holy Shruti confirmed by his own experience. The egoity of the disciple, which is the chief barrier between him and the ever-shining splendour of God-head in his Ātman, is thinned out by submission and surrender to the teacher. God is revealed as the Self.

Verse 51

viśīrṇa-kārya-karaṇo bhūta-sūkṣmair anāvṛtaḥ
vimukta-karma-nigaḍaḥ sadya eva vimucyate

All limitations of cause and effect having ended, unconditioned by the subtle and the gross bodies, no longer attached to the chain of action, the disciple is immediately liberated from nescience.

This verse describes the state of nirvāna which should constantly be reflected upon. A man can gauge the extent of his spiritual awakening by referring to the conditions contained in this verse. He is no longer subject to the law of cause and effect, which operates in the realm of relativity (māyā). He knows Ātman to be absolutely distinct from the physical and mental bodies and the vital airs. Liberation, like the dawn of the sun, comes all at once. A man does not feel it slowly creeping on him. It is not like the gradual emergence of the moon from a total eclipse. It is a sudden rush of reality-consciousness which overpowers the consciousness of relativity.

Jivan-mukti continues until prārabdha karma is exhausted.

Verse 52

prārabdha-karma-vegena jīvan-mukto yadā bhavet
kiñcit kālam ānārabdha-karma-bandhasya saṃkṣaye

After the destruction of those actions whose fruition has

not yet begun, the Jīvan-mukta lives on for a while, his life being maintained by the past karma which has begun to produce results (prārabdha karma).

In this verse the traditional view of the Jīvan-mukta's continued life in this world is explained on a relatively low basis for the good of aspirants in general. The doctrine of prārabdha karma is here accepted as a working hypothesis, although in other great classics it is not mentioned. Swami Sacchidananda did not endorse it, nor does Shri Shankara in other of his classics.

Then follows absolute liberation (Videha-mukti) and one is not reborn.

Verse 53

nirastātiśayānandaṃ vaiṣṇavaṃ paramaṃ padam
punar āvṛtti-rahitaṃ kaivalyaṃ pratipadyate

On completion of the fruit of the actions of prārabdha, the jñānī enters the state of absolute liberation. There is no further birth for him. He enjoys the unsurpassable bliss which is called the abode of Vishṇu.

When the impact of karma, the fruition of which has already begun, called prārabdha, is exhausted, the yogi enters into the blissful state of absolute liberation from sansāra and karma. It does not mean that there is any slight bondage still left for him. This doctrine of prārabdha is accepted to explain to the uninitiated the mystery of the continuation of the life of a Jīvan-mukta. From the highest point of view, liberation is liberation and there are no stages in it such as jīvan-mukti and release after death (videha-mukti). When the illusory snake disappears and the rope, its substratum, is revealed, the snake does not disappear by stages. You cannot say first the tail goes and then the teeth and the venomous hood. In the theory of Ajāta-vāda, which is accepted in the highest state of Vedānta, there is no such distinction as that between jīvan-mukti and videha-mukti.

The expression 'state of Vishṇu' does not mean any personal state. It is a reference to a passage in the Veda. The word 'Vishṇu' means the all-pervasive Lord and his bliss is the consciousness of man in its real aspect.

OM

SELECT GLOSSARY

Advaita doctrine
The Vedānta philosophy of Non-duality, which teaches that there is one Absolute Reality 'without a second', and that man's individual self (Ātman) is identical with this Supreme Spirit (Brahman).
Ajñāna, Avidyā
Spiritual ignorance or nescience.
Brahman
Absolute Reality, the attributeless and impersonal aspect of God.
Chārvāka
Materialist school of philosophy in ancient India.
Dharma
The moral and spiritual Law of right and harmonious living.
Īshvara
Personal God; the Lord of the Universe conceived as a being with whom man can enter into personal relationship.
Jīva, jīvātman
The individual soul or self.
Jīvan-mukta
One who has attained jīvan mukti.
Jīvan-mukti
Liberation from nescience (avidyā) when one's true identity with Ātman is intuitively realized. God-realization. Literally 'liberation while living', in contrast with a salvation that has its consummation after death (videha-mukti).
Manana
Conscious reflection on the spiritual teachings one has heard.

Māyā

The creative power of the Lord, by means of which the illusion of the phenomenal world has been brought into existence; the cosmic nescience which by its veiling power (āvarana shakti) hides the reality of the Self and by its projecting power (vikshepa shakti) gives rise to the belief that the manifested world is real.

Nididhyāsana

Spiritual contemplation, unbroken meditation.

Nyāyā

School of 'logician' philosophers in ancient India who depended on reasoning independent of scriptural revelation.

Paramātman

The supreme Self; Ātman considered as the Self of the universe.

Prakriti

Matter, Nature, the primordial substance out of which the physical and mental universe is composed.

Prārabdha karma

The past actions of an individual which have begun to produce their effects in the present life-time.

Purusha

Spirit, real Self. Like prakriti, a term characteristic of the Sāṅkhya philosophy.

Sāṅkhya

Philosophical school in ancient India, teaching a dualism of matter and spirit, yet sharing some doctrines with Advaita.

Samādhi

Higher spiritual concentration in which the subject-object division is transcended.

Sansara

Phenomenal world made up of name, form and action. Empirical experience. The cycle of rebirth.

Sattva
The purity, clarity and benevolence of the spiritualized intellect.
Shānti
Spiritual peace.
Shravana
Conscious hearing of the spiritual Truth with the aim of realizing it in one's own experience.
Shruti
The Vedas, particularly the Upanishads, considered as revealed scriptures.
Vākya
Sentence. Here stands for the text 'Tat tvam asi', 'That thou art', one of the four mahā-vākyas or 'great sentences' in the Vedas which proclaim the highest Truth of the identity of the individual self (jīva) and Brahman.
Vritti
Modification of the mind; thought. In **Vākya-Vritti** it denotes the 'meaning' or 'function' of the (great) sentence.

SHANTI SADAN PUBLICATIONS

THE HEART OF THE

EASTERN MYSTICAL TEACHING

'Every man must be able to go into voluntary mental and nervous relaxation, and concentrate his mind on a symbol of God, whether it be a word, a concept or an image. It is this prolonged silence of the soul which brings before man the patterns of what he is to create, the archetypes of his contribution to the inner and outer world.'

An account of the teachings and way of life of the spiritually illumined sage, Shri Dada of Aligarh (1854-1910).

The book provides answers to the intellectual problems and conflicts that face mankind, and is at the same time a presentation of the spiritual way of life which is the greatest contribution India can make to the West.

Those seeking insight and assurance about the mystical techniques of the East will find authoritative guidance in these pages, from one who was convinced that all true religions lead to the same goal - the discovery of infinite peace as one's own higher Self.

450 pp paperback

978-0-85424-030-2

SHANTI SADAN PUBLICATIONS

Original works by Hari Prasad Shastri

The Heart of the Eastern Mystical Teaching

The Search for a Guru

Wisdom from the East

Meditation Its Theory and Practice

Yoga (Foyles Handbook)

A Path to God-Realization

Vedanta Light   Echoes of Japan

Scientist and Mahatma

Spring Showers (poems)

* * *

Translations of philosophical and spiritual classics

The Ramayana of Valmiki (3 volumes)

Ashtavakra Gita   Avadhut Gita

Direct Experience of Reality

Teachings from the Bhagavad Gita

Triumph of a Hero

Verses from the Upanishads

Panchadashi

World Within the Mind (from Yoga Vasishtha)

SHANTI SADAN PUBLICATIONS

Books by Marjorie Waterhouse

Power Behind the Mind
Training the Mind through Yoga
What Yoga Has to Offer

* * *

Books by A M Halliday

Freedom through Self-Realisation
Yoga for the Modern World
The Spiritual Awakening of Science

* * *

Shankara Studies
A Shankara Source Book (in six volumes)
compiled and translated by Dr A J Alston

* * *

SELF-KNOWLEDGE Yoga Quarterly
devoted to spiritual thought and practice

* * *